My Little Word Books

D0503503

HAMPTON-BROWN

Contents

How to Assemble:

1

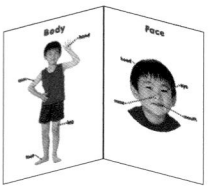

1. Tear one sheet off at perforation.
2. Fold on solid line.

2

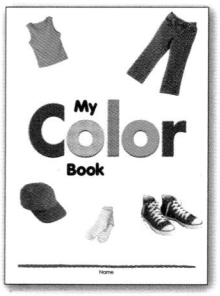

1. Tear two sheets off at perforation.
2. Fold both sheets together on solid line.
3. Staple along folded edge.
4. Cut interior pages only along dashed lines.

3

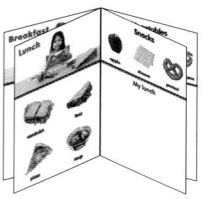

1. Tear two sheets off at perforation.
2. Fold both sheets together on solid line.
3. Staple along folded edge.

4

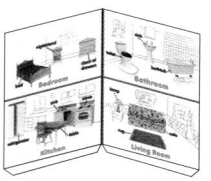

1. Tear one sheet off at perforation.
2. Cut out triangle at bottom along dashed lines.
3. Fold bottom of sheet on solid line, toward side that shows interior of home. This will allow folded sheet to stand up.

5

1. Tear three sheets off at perforation.
2. Fold all three sheets together on solid line.
3. Staple along folded edge.

How to Assemble:

6

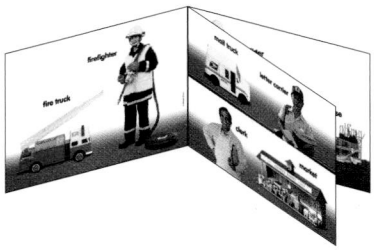

1. Tear three sheets off at perforation.
2. Staple together at left edge.

7

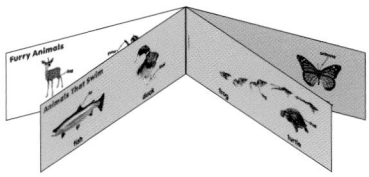

1. Tear two sheets off at perforation.
2. Cut each sheet in half along dashed line.
3. Stack resulting strips in this order, top to bottom: cover—bear/skunk—frog/turtle—bee/butterfly.
4. Staple together at left edge.

8

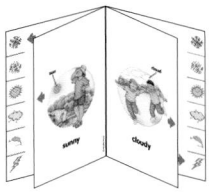

1. Tear two sheets off at perforation.
2. Fold both sheets together on solid line.
3. Staple along folded edge.
4. Cut **interior pages only** along dashed lines.

9

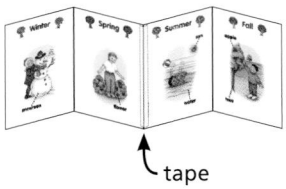

1. Tear one sheet off at perforation.
2. Cut in half along dashed line.
3. Fold each piece in half as shown.
4. Tape together to make accordion book.

10

1. Tear three sheets off at perforation.
2. Fold all three sheets together on solid line.
3. Staple along folded edge.

My foot

© Hampton-Brown

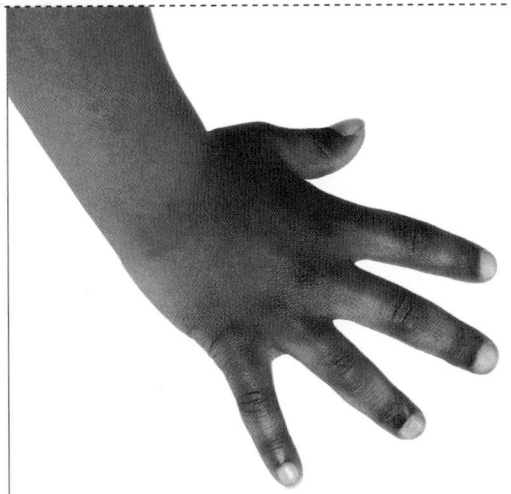

My Body Book

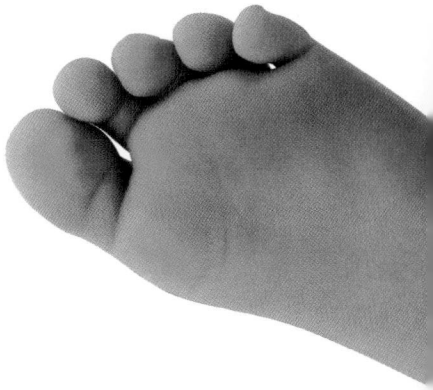

Name

Body

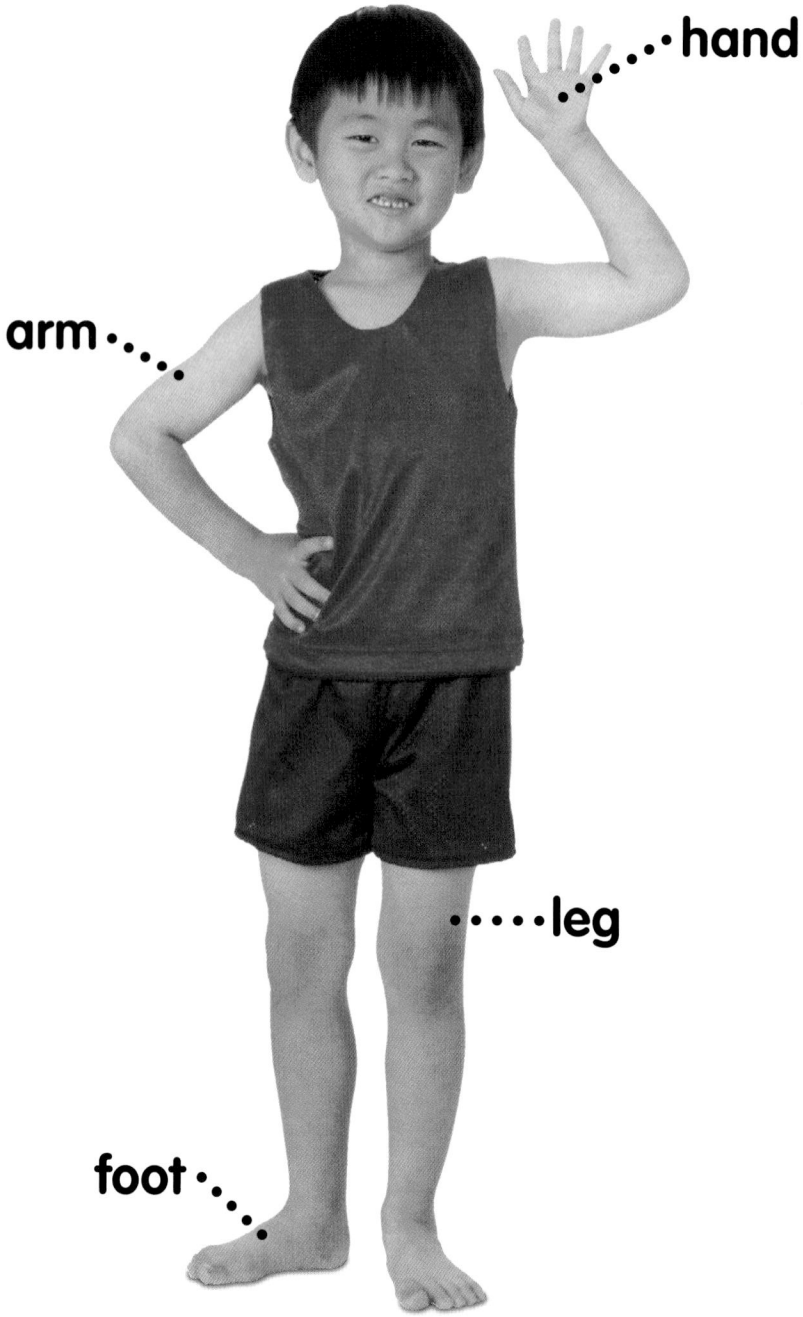

Face

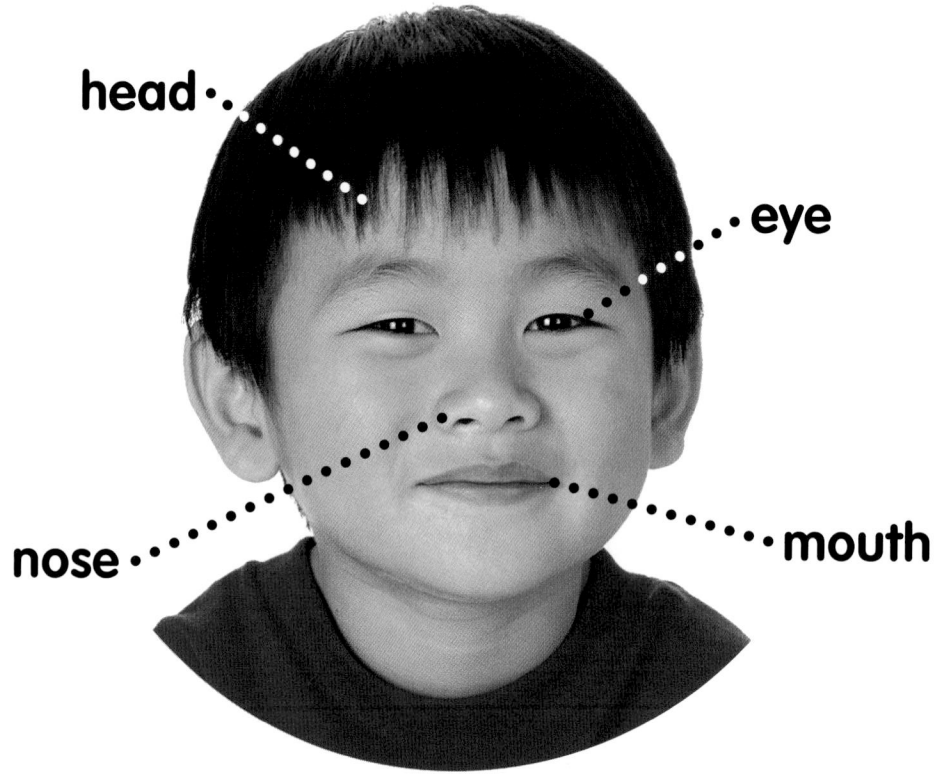

My favorite color

© Hampton-Brown

My Color Book

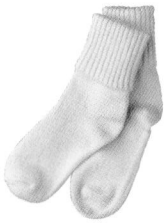

Name

green

red

green

red

blue

blue

© Hampton-Brown

orange

orange

yellow

purple

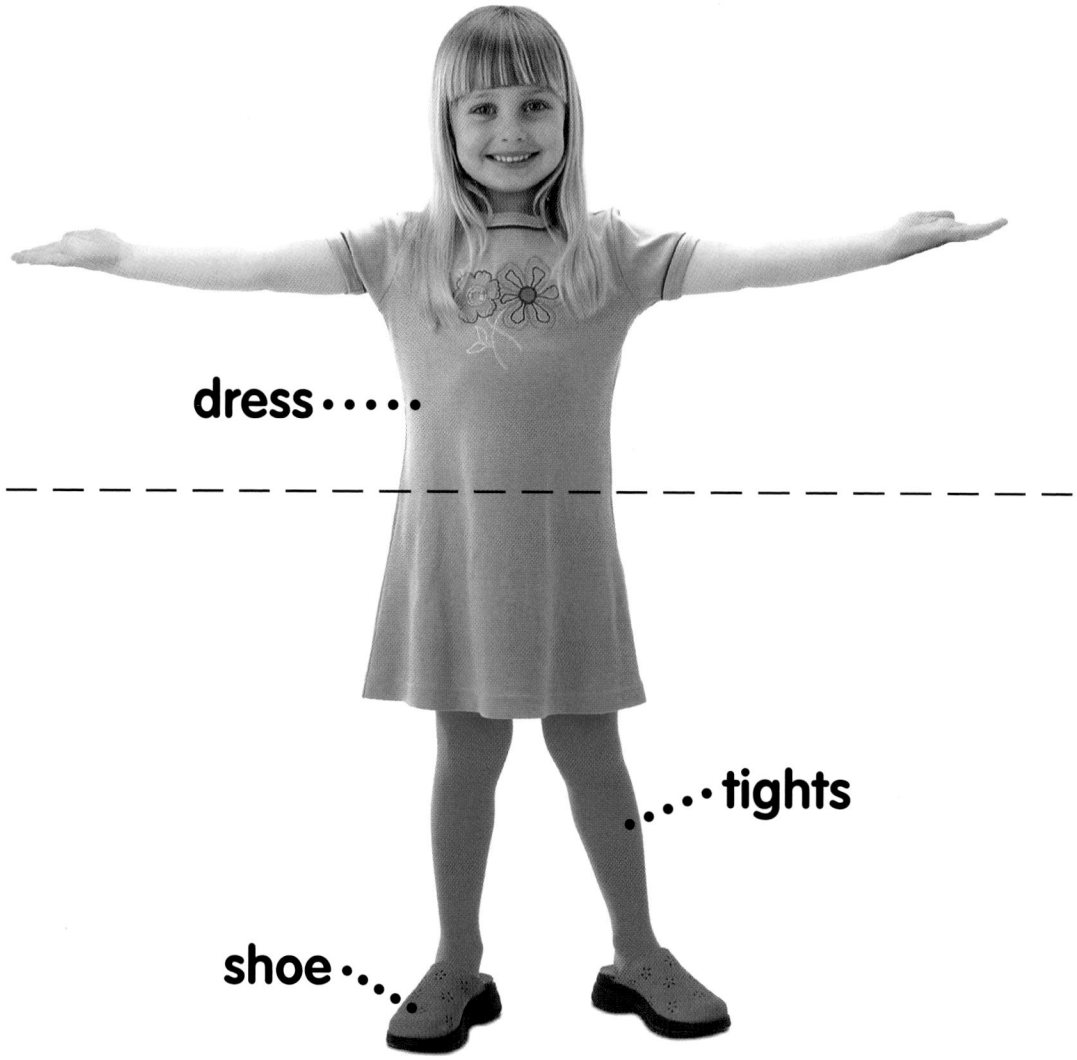

yellow

purple

Dessert

fresh fruit

cookies

rice pudding

cake

ice cream

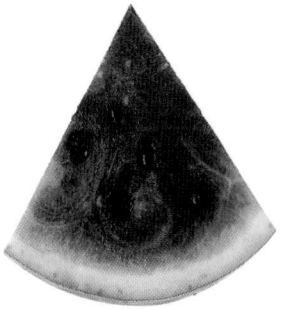

watermelon

© Hampton-Brown

My Food Book

Name

Breakfast

Vegetables

salad

broccoli

string beans

cereal

bread

bagel

banana

My dinner

Dinner

chicken and rice

beans

tortillas

salsa

© Hampton-Brown

Drinks

milk

orange juice

water

My breakfast

Lunch

Snacks

apple

cheese

pretzel

My lunch

sandwich

taco

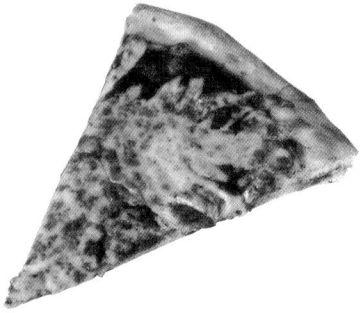

pizza

soup

In my home

bed

lamp

sink

table

rug

sofa

© Hampton-Brown

My Home Book

Name

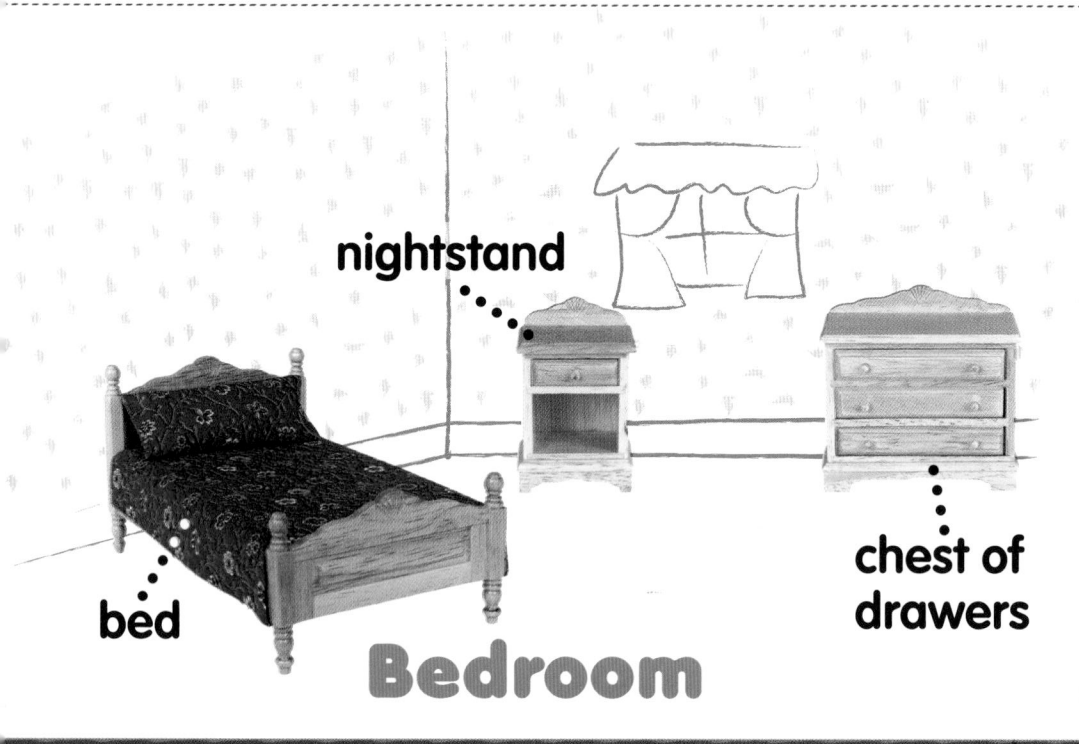
nightstand
bed
chest of drawers
Bedroom

sink
toilet
bathtub
Bathroom

sink
stove
refrigerator
table
Kitchen

lamp
sofa
rug
Living Room

My family

My Family Book

Name

grandpa and grandma

© Hampton-Brown

Knock, knock!
Who's there?

mother and baby

Knock, knock!
Who's there?

sister and brother

© Hampton-Brown

Knock, knock!
Who's there?

father

My Neighborhood Book

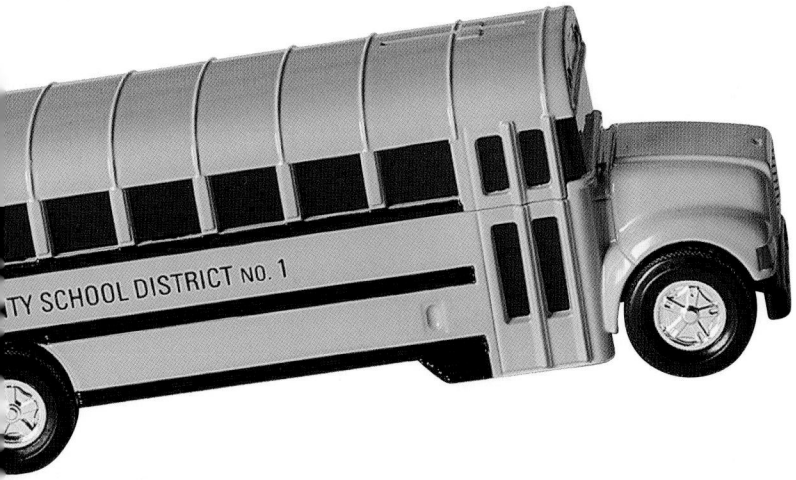

Name

© Hampton-Brown

mail truck
UNITED STATES POSTAL SERVICE
letter carrier
clerk
market
FRUIT
FARMER'S MARKET
PRODUCE

© Hampton-Brown

builder
house
dump truck

Drive the to the .
FARMER'S MARKET
POLICE STATION
FIRE STATION 3
POST OFFICE
POLICE
DIAL 911
FRUIT
FARMER'S MARKET
PRODUCE
© Hampton-Brown

My Animal Book

Name

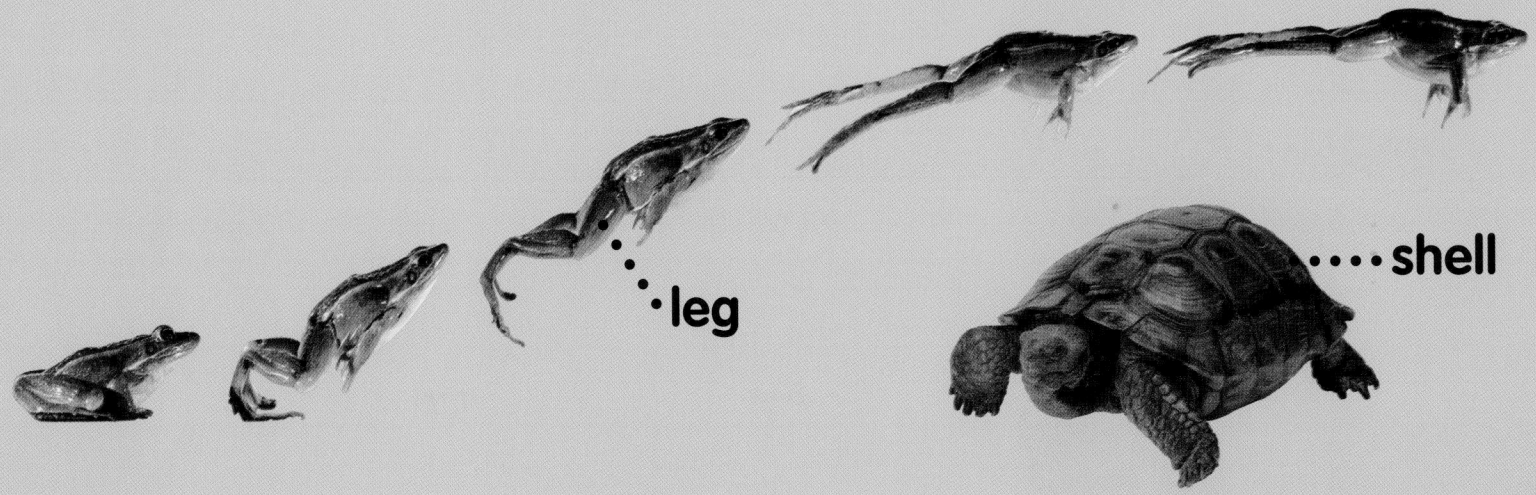

frog

turtle

© Hampton-Brown

Furry Animals

deer

raccoon

Animals That Fly

eagle

woodpecker

© Hampton-Brown

bear

skunk

bee

butterfly

© Hampton-Brown

Animals That Swim

fish

duck

Find 6 animals in the forest.

© Hampton-Brown

windy

© Hampton-Brown

rainy

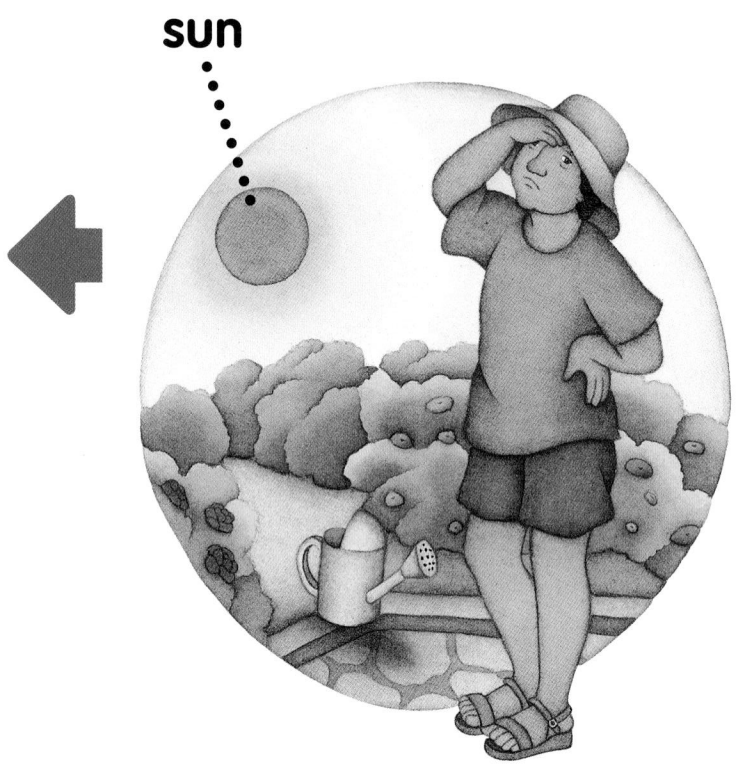

sunny

cloudy

© Hampton-Brown

My Seasons Book

Name

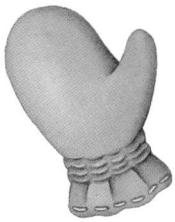

Match.

Winter

Spring

Summer

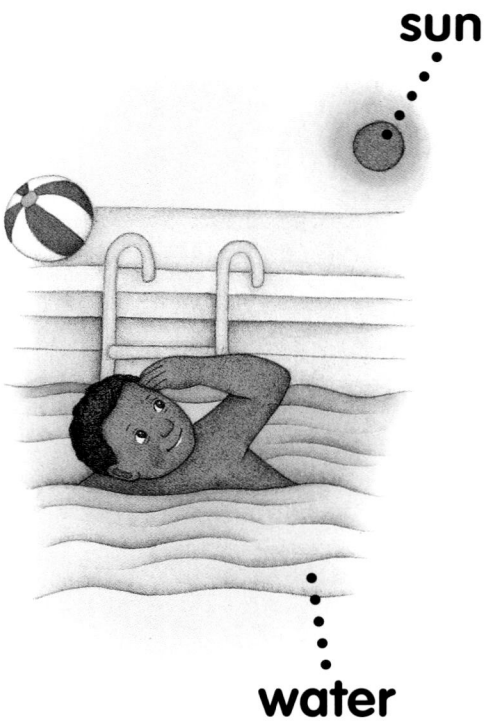

Fall

© Hampton-Brown

Color the plant.

green

yellow

red

© Hampton-Brown

My Plant Book

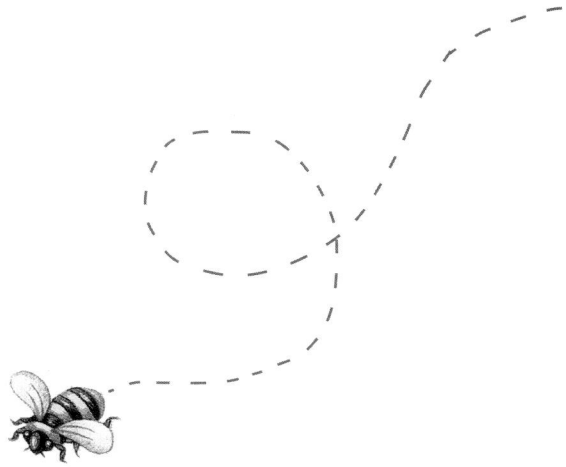

Name

1 seed

10 pods

Picking

9 ladybugs

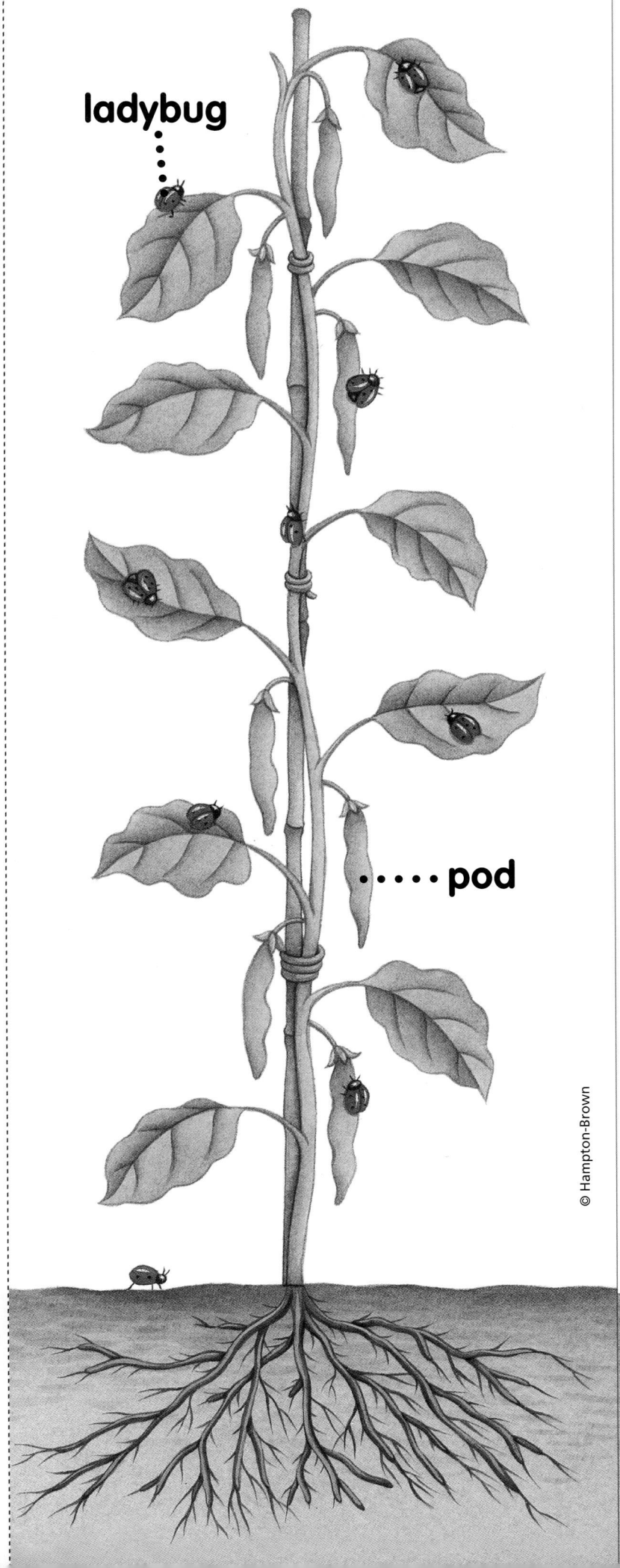

© Hampton-Brown

2 birds

Planting

3 worms

8 butterflies

Digging

7 flowers
flower
© Hampton-Brown
4 bees
bee
Watering

5 leaves

6 weeds

Weeding